Written By:
Michael Broell
Original Art
By: Billy Evans

PublishAmerica
Baltimore

First printing

ISBN: 978-1-4560-2928-9
PUBLISHED BY PUBLISHAMERICA, LLLP
www.publishamerica.com
Baltimore

Printed in the United States of America

PREFACE

The following pages contain some of the Fine Art of

Billy Evans, Evans Gallery, Carmel by the Sea, California.

Recently Billy decided to partner with Michael Broell (poet, writer) to combine children's rhyming verse with some of his art, creating:

The Child's Fine Art Book in Verse

Billy Evans - Painter & Sculptor

Mr. Evans did his undergraduate art studies at the Massachusetts College of Art in Boston. His art is in the collections of numerous museums in the U.S. His gallery is located in the renowned art community of Carmel by the Sea, California.

Michael Broell - Author

While writing, Mr. Broell studied and lectured in the U.S., Europe, India, Pakistan and Iran, relating to Eastern Philosophy and Human Development.

We Acknowledge with warm appreciation,
Wendy Nankervis for her valuable support in critiquing the verses in this book . . . thank you Wink.

This book is Dedicated to Billy and Michael's children and grand children (ages 2 to 29): Keetsa, Keeley, Nicole, Jesse, Kaylynn, Jay Jay, Kole, Peyton, Marley and Rylie

INTRODUCTION

Welcome to the art of Billy Evans, Evans Gallery, Carmel by the Sea, California. This is the first book from Billy Evans and Michael Broell in an effort to introduce fine art to children in verse form. Please do read it to the children, patiently waiting to see their response and their comments. Never hesitate to explain the art images (verse related) if the child seems not to understand. While reading to them, pointing to birds, cats, sailboats, etc., is very valuable for very young children, as you may well know.

We are optimistic that you, your children, grandchildren or preschool students, will find this book entertaining, art educational, visually and verbally uplifting. When Dr. Seuss (Theodor Geisel) wrote his book, The Cat in The Hat, in 1957, It was revolutionary in its approach to child education. We sincerely hope that our book will be at least somewhat pioneering in terms of introducing children to Fine Art in verse beyond illustrations and figurative art.

See if your child might enjoy a favorite art image from the book on their bedroom wall . . . or for Mom and Dad, on some wall in the home ?

Any of the art pieces included in this book can be ordered in the sizes and prices listed below:
11x14 - Giclee Reproduction (Archival Paper and Inks) - **$90**
22x30 - Giclee Reproduction (Archival Paper and Inks) - **$190**
Shipping and Handling - $10.00 or $15.00 per shipment.

Originals and Canvas Reproductions are available upon request.

For Ordering Contact: Billy Evans - Artist - **(831) 238-6747**

Warm Regards,

Michael Broell & Billy Evans

To view more Evans art images see: www.evansgallery.org

Also see: www.catsevansgallery.org for **CAT ART**

Chirp, Chirp, Chirp . . . excuse me if I burp. Please listen to me . . . I am the bird in the tree.

We are so pink . . . do you think our feet stink? Thanks for saying no . . . we will stay and never go.

It is so nice to see you 2 kitties . . . wow! But please stay right where you are now!

That is such a sleepy cat. He just eats and poohs and naps. Thanks that he is nice and thanks that we're not mice.

I am the white kitty, and my sister kitty is black. Please Mommy, it's time for me to sit on your lap.

Ring around the flower chair. We love to play together out there. We are brother and sister, family pets. We love each other, as good as it gets.

Peek a Boo . . . I love to play games with you. Please don't fall . . . I need you more than all.

Birdie did you invite again the cat? Yes I did Sweetie, for she is lonely, so that is that!

It is magic coming out of the pot!! Do you see it . . . do you believe it or not??

We are the lovely peaches on a lovely peach chair, with baby birds most everywhere. But would you kindly put us back, upon the table where we once joy-fully sat?

I am a good kitty, watching the fish on my back. But do they love me, and are they looking back?

I'm the orange bird
all alone on top of the
chair. The family is
sailing, but I don't care.
I love to eat peaches
right out of the bowls;
I just hope that Mom
won't see the holes.

The family is out, so I am happy to sit by myself on the table . . . but Dad will not like it.

We love the bridge and river, and also the trees. So Daddy, take us all floating out to the seas.

So many happy birds, together in the court yard. Are there 7 or 8? Sometimes counting is hard.

What a beautiful day! I stopped bicycling to go swim. Please come join me . . . I hope you will jump in.

It is just us . . . two pink birds . . . husband and wife.
We love each other and the birch trees, all of our life.

Sweet, happy fishes
swimming so friendly
in their fish bowl.
They love each other's
company, as long as the
bowl has no leaky hole.

I am a loving hill-top tree, with my 2 growing kids. We are a good family . . . trunk, branches and twigs.

3 happy sail boats with 3 pretty birds and 1 silent cat. No . . . I am wrong . . . where is the 4th, big birdie at?

Spring is so nice, all the flower buds are on the trees.
Birdie, I'm so glad we met, always stay with me please.

I sure like driving in the car with my dad and my mom.
But may we drop my brother off at the next farm?

Here sit 5 beautiful Cockatiel birds; so happy you see.
You can teach them to talk, just like mine talks to me.

The butterflies are flying happy together with color.
Which do you see as father, mother, sister or brother?

From our house, I watch the small boat coming to shore.
They were out fishing; have you ever done that before?

I am happy on this chair,
even with no one over there.
But I would be oh so happy
with you in the other chair.

Bye, Bye
. . . sorry
but we
have to
fly . . .
it's time
for alarm!
Kitty is up
our tree
. . . do
you think
he means
us harm?

Roosters rule the barnyard over all of the chicken hens. . . so it is said. But I think the chicken hens are so many, so they rule roosters instead.

I'm a molded kitty half asleep with bird and mouse. My tail-bird and my book-mouse, love rhyming verse. I read them bed-time stories, but I fall asleep first.

I am also a molded kitty balancing 3 mice. 1 is on my tail and 2 are on sticks. If they all 3 fall, it will be a playful mousey mix.

Sometimes flowers look like butterflies floating in air.
They are so happy with each other . . . no worry or care.

7 white birdies around the flower table and chairs. Most are talking, but 2 are kissing . . . you tell me where?

Time to have a tea party . . . come sit with me please.
There is milk and sugar . . . but please do not sneeze.

Here are bright colored tulips . . . flowers you can find.
For fun, I call them TWO LIPS . . . yours and mine.

A silent black kitty is looking out a big window, in her most favorite place. Behind her is a lovely little table with tiny pink flowers in a cute little vase.

I wonder if someone is crossing that bridge over there. Do they think of jumping in and swimming back here?

What a colorful sunset reflecting on the lake! Quick, let's all go watch, before it's too late!

There go Mom and Dad out sailing in their 2 sail boats . . . just off the beach.

Gramma is going to make sliced peaches, with whipped cream, for us kids to eat.

Look at me . . . I am the red butterfly on top of the lemon. I keep the banana, plate and cups from falling . . . or they will start howling and bawling.

See all the green birds behind the flowers and chairs? They want kids to sit and talk, about anything . . . even lions and tigers and bears.

Such a black cat, sleeping upon a black table top. He's missing the colors outside . . . he's such a kitty flop.

What an orange sunset on all the hills in the breeze. Mommy, may we go picnic there some day, please?

That's weird . . . 2 bananas stuck in a plate! The fruit is happy to be there, as breakfast or dessert can wait.

I feel so pretty . . . don't you think you are just as pretty, even without a beak? Someone left this bowl for me to drink. That is much better than drinking from the sink.

Let's say good night, Birdie love . . . my eyes are closing.
It is so special to be a bird, and not need clothing.

Now that looks wild . . . don't you think? It must be from the ocean, and maybe it stinks? You smell it first and then I will follow. You can lick it . . . but do not swallow!

Such a pretty white tree . . . looks like Christmas time.
It's not, but I'll take a present . . . would you be so kind?

Baby, listen to your mother and get down from that rail. Don't make me come over there and pull you down, by your little kitty tail!

Humming Birds can fly upside down, anyway and anywhere.
This one's happy drinking flower nectar . . . just right there.

Daddy, do you see that hand holding a branch with 4 birdies sitting on it? Yes Honey . . . the hand is helping them, and hoping they won't pooh on it.

I love the view of that blue balcony onto the sea. The cats and birds aren't around, happy not to be found.

Wow . . . Holy Cow; what is that thing anyhow? Looks to me like it's something from the sea, or maybe something from a tree? Oh my . . . what could it be?

Where will this road take us camping today? We have our tent and food . . . it is so nice to get away.

Those flowers are called LILLIES . . . at least I think. When it rains they catch water for the birds to drink.

Mommy, Daddy, who do you think lives in that cabin?
Could it be an ogre . . . an angel . . . or even a dragon!?

Here comes Grampa, home from all day fishing.
Sometimes he likes being alone, just fishy wishing.

You see the 11 butterflies, flying in different ways. So pretty, yet sad, as they most only live about 11 days.

There go 5 of those guys flying together like planes. They are flying in lines like a family as one . . . beyond any pains.

The fishes are swimming all alone at home in their motion . . . I wonder if they are watching the flowers and the clouds and the ocean?

2 white boats? Or maybe 2 white birds? Heading into the sky. The flowers and peaches know which . . . but are just too shy.

Happy Mother's Day Mommy!! We sure hope you like the flowers. Dad took us to the store, and we got so bored . . . it seemed to take him hours.

Here are the flowers that we kids chose best on our own. But you know Dad . . . so we said yes, and just headed home.

Look . . . it's another chair with fruit! I don't mind, it's just fine. I like eating fruit. Lucky it's not a bean burrito . . . that makes me rooty, toot, toot.

#1 birdie said to birdie #2 . . . do you read books? #2 birdie said no . . . I listen and just give sweet looks.

Oh Wow, what is that . . . 3 cups and 2 dishes standing perfectly still? It must be a miracle, or it could be that flower stem, holding them together like a hill?

How did a banana get stuck in a plate . . . please explain? Maybe 2 pears put it there, to protect them from rain?

I think those birds are pink? But we cats see better at night. So those birdies better take flight at night; because we can catch them without much fight.

I feel pretty, oh so pretty . . . and so do my lovely birds.
I can't put my love for them into, just colorful and flowery words.

Hey, Hey, Hey, look down; I'm the brown small kitty about to fall to the ground! Come on and give me a helping paw . . . Mom or Dad or Granma or Grampa!

I am the one Birdie . . . I can fly . . . and you can't. Please listen to me and help that little kitty cat, before she falls, and we never find where she is at.

Sweet petite butterfly . . . I so want to play with you! You are so quick that I can never ever catch you. Maybe some day we will run so free, through the flowers with you chasing me.

I am a lover cat in a bed of flowers. I can lie here happy, in sunshine or showers. How about you . . . what makes you happy for hours?

WINTER is coming and now is the season they call FALL. SUMMER is gone and the leaves are beginning to fall. They are changing colors, and then comes SPRING . . . my favorite of all.

Now my favorite season SPRING has come! The leaves are green & the buds are pink & white. The days are so alive and filled with sunlight . . . so much fun with friends, playing together, into night.

OMG . . . Oh My Goodness; just look out into that yard, and then look back onto 2 black kitty cats! They are small but are "living large". I love being here . . . though sometimes what I dearly wish is to also have a dog, a bird and a fish.

LOL . . . Lots of Love my baby kitty. So your friend left you?
He will be back, of that I am sure. I am here with you, with my love . . . and love is always a magic cure.

Birds all seem to love me . . . don't they love you too?
The puff flowers all surround me.
They guide the birds to come down from their tree . . .
to perch upon me.

What a great day!
I am so happy you guys always come my way.
I have 3 Birdies and 2 Kitties who sleep more than play.
Is it OK if we just stay here, all together . . . forever and a day?

Pretty Birdies, you can trust me . . . so come down from that tree . . . I am a good Kitty. OH NO, good Kitty . . . though you are pretty, please be true . . . because we don't trust you . . . any more than we can throw you.

I see you, so you must see me . . . you 3 Birdies up there in that tree. I will open the window so you can fly to me. I love you a bunch! We can have such fun with you as my guests and you as my lunch.

Do you see the bridge and its reflection upon the water . . . like a glass sea? It's like looking into a mirror, because it makes you wonder . . . is there just one, or two of me?

Early one morning, I saw a maiden watering the flowers as they grow. Some grew so fast, some might never last, and then some almost live forever . . . in good or even nasty weather.

Row, Row, Row your boat . . .
it's not as easy as it seems. Our dad is so good at doing it, and so happy just to row and sit; surrounded by so many colors and outdoor dreams.

Just the two of us, my boy and me, rowing back from that stormy sea. What a cool, fun day, in such a rainy way; in our sea-going caps with waves that slap the oars taking us back to the shores . . . where Mom is making us oodles of S'mores.

Where did those guys go who were in that boat? The boat is still afloat; maybe it just drifted loose from the shore? That's fine, never mind. I love the reflection, of the sky, trees and hills upon the lake and so much more.

The water does not move, and there is no wind. The day is at an end.
All the birds are silent. It's just me and my little lonely boat.
I wish the kids were here with me afloat.
But it's now time to row back to home . . . where I am never alone.